a guide to community discovery

22 WAYS TO HEAL US

FELICIA GUY-LYNCH

Dedication

To all those striving to heal and maintain salvation.

Thank you Melissa McLetchie for inspiring this edition!

Rest in Peace While You're Still Alive

Because if you stay woke all the time, you will get a bag under your third eye.
You gotta chill.

check out: sleepfoundation.org

Create a Social Stratosphere

It's good to know who your go-tos are in the time of need.
Family isn't always blood.

write 'em down

Acknowledge Post Partum Depression

Fellas! Yes. I'm talking to you!
The mother of your child is *not* the only one prone to this.
You are prone to this as well and that's ok.
Unpack whatever overwhelms you about fatherhood.
We need you King.

check out: therapyforblackmen.org

Self-Care

You can only tend to the people and things that you love as
good as you tend to yourself.
The first law of nature is self-preservation.
It's not the same as being selfish.

check out: verywellmind.com

Reintegrate

They say it takes a village to raise a child.
It also takes a village to assist them upon release.
Don't try this alone.
Everybody needs somebody.
Even the most independent soul needs trusted allies.

check out: blackyouthjobs.com

Budget

Your time. Unlike money, you can't get it back.
Take your time but don't waste it.
Use it wisely.

check out: skillsyouneed.com

Play a
Board Game

Give the apps on your phone a break.
Make it a family night if everyone is willing to make time.

check out: boardgamebliss.com

Embrace
Minimalism

Or at least try to by finding what you can donate or sell
to create more space for yourself

check out: becomingminimalist.com

Stock Up

You save money and make fewer trips to the store. Plus, you get an added sense of security knowing you have your essentials.

check out: good2goco.ca

Homeschool

One of the benefits is being able to tailor the education to your child's and/or youth's learning style and personality

check out: familyeducation.com

Learn a New Skill

Boost your employability or start a side hustle

check out: udemy.com

Explain Why

Just telling them no isn't enough

check out: todaysparent.com

Set
Boundaries

Part of how people treat you is based on how you let them

check out: psychologytoday.com

Take Advantage of Workplace Benefits

check with your employer

See if you have an Employee Assistance Plan.
If so, you can book a counselling session and talk to a
professional to get some unbiased advice.

Accept Their Collect Calls

It's hard enough being locked up.
You can help make their stay more bearable.

be present

Go Visit Them

Whether it's a correctional facility or a long term care residence, human touch is irreplaceable.
If you're not able to make physical contact, FaceTime them!

check out: zoom.us

Stretch

Relieve some tension you didn't know you were holding onto

check out: verywellfit.com

Pillow Talk

Take a break from scrolling and ask your partner how
their day went.
That way, you minimize the chances of them feeling
neglected.

Go on Walks Together

If you're too tired for pillow talk, schedule some time for outdoors.
Helps with fitness too.

hold hands

Read a Bedtime Story

It helps to foster your young one's imagination

check out: parents.com

Cook

Give Uber Eats a break or if you're that lazy, order cooked food
from a local restaurant.
Try cheffin' it up with the young one's if you do end up in the
kitchen.

check out: foodnetwork.com

Brainstorm

Whether you're trying to figure out what to eat or setting
goals, this helps with the process of elimination.
It also helps give clarity before arriving at a final decision.

check out: mindtools.com